Twenty-Four

A Glimpse of My Heart and Life

Shaena Jones
Queen J

Copyright © 2019 by Shaena Jones
Twenty-Four
A Glimpse Of My Heart And Life

All rights reserved. In accordance with the U.S. Copyright Act of 1976, the scanning, uploading, and electronic sharing of any part of this book without the permission of the publisher is unlawful piracy and theft of the author's intellectual property. If you would like to use material from the book, prior written permission must be obtained by contacting the publisher at
info@entegritypublishing.com.

Thank you for your support of the author's rights.
Entegrity Choice Publishing
PO Box 453
Powder Springs, GA 30127
info@entegritypublishing.com
www.entegritypublishing.com
770.727.6517

Printed in the United States of America

The views expressed in this work are solely those of the author and do not necessarily reflect the views of the publisher, and the publisher hereby disclaims any responsibility for them. The publisher is not responsible for websites (or their content) that are not owned by the publisher.

Library of Congress Cataloging-in-Publication Data
ISBN 978-1-7325767-6-6
Library of Congress Control Number: 2018964884

Twenty-Four

A Glimpse of My Heart and Life

The Love of My Life - GOD

Thank you for everything you have showered over my life which includes the love that you have shown me, the care, the support, and for pushing me when I am down and out. The days you showed me at twenty-four, I will hide in my heart forever, never to be erased.

I could spend days, weeks, months…recounting over and over the times you saved my life with your grace, love and mercy. Thank you for awakening my sleeping mind while I was in auto pilot, risking my entire life while you stood firm as my shield, my light, my strength and my refuge.

Your Favorite Daughter,
Shaena, Queen J

Grandstand to the year that you changed my NAME
Twenty-Four

Dedication

This book is dedicated to my wonderful oldest sister, Shantel Bussey, for her strength, courage, and resilience. Even when she doesn't know that I'm watching, I admire her from afar. I push you so much because you are an amazing person with lots to offer this WORLD. I love you.

Heartfelt dedication to my second oldest sister, Wanita Bussey. Appreciate you for being exactly like me and showing me that I am different from other people, but it's okay because I'll have you. Girl, realizing we are so much alike has REALLY been amazing. It is a joy to have a sister like you that I can be myself around you, you are my SHERO.

To my best friend Johnny Jones, my brother, for being forgiving enough to move forward. You are an amazing person and so many people love you. You are never alone because I love you, and so does the world. I know you are here for me and I want you to know how proud I am to be your baby sister. Even in the hardest of times, I watched you cry and get back up.

Love always
Baby Sis
Shaena

Vanita & Queen

To my biological mother, Vanita Jones, I honor you for being a beautiful soul who reminds me daily that life is worth living. I love you forever Mom. Thank you for your continued fight.

Ophelia & Queen

Mom, this is loving memory of YOU. I will NEVER be able to repay you for your love. I will carry in my heart forever all the lessons. It's not everyday people are blessed the way that I have been. I am grateful to God for saving a place in your heart for you to love me.

Cousin Jackie said, "Precious memories, oh how they linger." How true is that statement. I know things change and such is life but your departing from this world has changed my life. Thank you again for always being with me and being bold enough even when they told you not to send me home. YOU BELIEVED IN ME. You saw what the world didn't. You saw Me - your baby girl.

David, the question of life is not why, but when and how. Love found us and we made the most of it the way that we both knew how. I am thankful to you for being one of my closest friends even when I don't stop to acknowledge. My supporter and even my love! You are an amazing person and if you keep on, you are going to shock the entire world "NERD".

Noah and Elijah: the love, light and strength that you guys have brought to my world will forever be appreciated. I am thankful to have loved and nurtured you boys. I know that life will take you far if you dream big and work smart.

Noah - Outsmart them and show the world who you are.

Elijah - Let me see you Dunk it.

Lastly, I salute myself, the 24 year old me…GIRL YOU DID AMAZING!

Contents

The Love of My Life 3
Dedication 5
Purpose 13
Twenty-Three 17
Strength 19
Biologically 21
Fostered 23
A Mother's Heart 25
Need 'A (Nita) 26
Suicide 28
Quanelias 31
Journey 33
Poison 35
Without You 37
Voice 38
Imagination 40
Doubt 42
Dream 43
Past 46
Socially Oblivious 48

The Waiting Room	49
Empty	50
That Day	51
Start	52
Knowledge	53
Speaks Wisdom	55
Valuable	56
Self-Discovery	58
For You	60
Awaken	61
Until Next Time	63
My Cousin, Mr. ShaQue Jones	64
Twenty-Four Days of Reflection	65
What I Wish I Knew at Twenty Four?	85
What's Happening 24?	89

Purpose

I used to dream of the things I could become. I idolized those who were living their life with a purpose. Envy is a better word, even though I know it's wrong, I was downright jealous. I wasn't sure how to pursue my dreams or where to begin. I didn't understand that I needed to look within to find my life's purpose. Though many people have told me my life was destined for greatness, I always listened to those tiny voices that told me what I couldn't become, because of where I had come from. It has taken me almost an entire decade to begin to heal.

I look at myself in the mirror now and I am proud of the woman I've managed to become. Writing has always been my outlet. Writing lets my spirit man roam free. I sit around pouring what comes from my heart in hopes that my message finds the person it's intended for.

I have experienced so many things: foster child, ADHD, criminal, out of control teen looking for love through men and sex, pregnant teen, drunken person with a sweetened sober soul, and a divorced single mother. Had it not been for those experiences, I would not be able to fulfill my life's purpose.

When I look in the mirror, I'm reminded of where I want to be. I've learned to find the lesson in everything and to use my voice to change the things I see. I believe we all have a power, but we must be willing to use it. There is a time for it to manifest which is the season in where you will endure. The season that you begin to understand and use that power will put you at your best. Through all of my life experiences I've found strength in having faith, believing that tomorrow would bring about a better day.

As I share with you my story, understand that I have something special to share. The day I realized that I was at my worse was the best day of my life because I chose to work on my God given Gift. I made a choice to change my life. I don't want to show my children how to be a quitter but to have resilience when all else fails, to bounce back even harder.

I have managed to take so many losses within the last two years. When my mother passed, I set out on a quest to have a beautiful relationship with my biological mother. To be more active rather than reactive. I lost my husband to "the system" and was forced to face divorce. This made me desire to actually find myself.

People wondered why I wanted to leave home. I wanted to leave because I needed to find me and what was important. As you read through these pages, relax and enjoy. My life is an open book.

I pray this book will help those that are lost find the light that shines within and stay motivated. No matter what lemons life gives; make the sweetest lemonade and move forward. There will be times you may not understand why "life happens", but if you hang in there, I'm sure your story will have a beautiful end.

Normally, ages 13, 21, 25, 30 and 50 are super significant. In my culture it tends to signify that we are at milestones. I finally understood that life was so much bigger than I thought. When my foster mother who raised me was called home, I had to figure life out for myself. At age 23, I began to see life differently and set out on my own path to understand myself. As I began searching for the answers I needed, I was drawn towards writing, something I have done since high school.

In this book, you will be brought into my mind, heart, body and soul. It is my intent to expose your mind to realities that some may not be aware of. Here are the Lessons that have helped me to become a better woman and mother at twenty-four. So, let's explore my life at twenty-four.

Get organized and get ready.

Do what makes you happy.

Success comes from effort.

Stay true to yourself.

Yours truly,
An African American Woman
Queen J

**"The modern-day Harriet Tubman
and Maya Angelou mixed in one"**

Twenty-Three

There I was a single mother
"Yea, that was me"
Faced with life's greatest challenge.

My mother was gone on
And me
I was alone you see.

Didn't know in which direction to turn
Couldn't figure it out
Life had just handed me a reality check
That I was not ready to cash.

Twenty-three years ago
She had come and rescued me
Now she was gone
So suddenly.

I know God has truly sent me one of
his most precious angels
Having to endure
Remain strong
While eyes were no doubt piercing
Bleeding holes into my soul.

When asked
"How are you holding up "
I'd remember more of what I truly wanted to forget
I had yet to wake up .
How could this happen?
What was to become?

Strength

As my support system shrank
I had to find new ways to see my strength
How to remain strong in the face of Adversity.

Dreams of a winner but it all seemed to be inside
What's the next step?
Help save young lives?
Destiny was pulling me
Couldn't figure out where to start.

Caregiving to my children was what seemed most important
Life was changing
Recently divorced
New city and single
With a list full of goals
Don't mean to be repetitive
But that's the way my story goes.

Was this God's plan to?
Eliminate distractions?
Changes were happening all around me
All I could do was smile.

I wasn't who I was last year right now
Seemed happy
A little confused
Deep inside there was a frown
I had taken my children from their families.
Mommy had to find what mattered most
Inner strength was being tested
Questions did arise
Do I turn back now?
Or keep pressing toward my prize?

Biologically

I never had a lick
Cause my mother was always sick
Busy drinking or smoking
My earthly father
There's no need to mention him.

But I am blessed
Raised with a family
Where love was the foundation
Christ was our leader.

They want me to be silent about my life
But no, it's gonna be spoken
Biologically, my blood lines are broken
Didn't grow up together and
Without them knowing
How it felt to be
Functional
Something that needs to be experienced.

How could we build something?
For the future
Feeling responsible
For our future generations
As a family

Maybe we need to do better.

A lot is left
Unspoken
Facebook friends
With our very cousins
Still our family left unawaken.

To the brokenness
We'd grown accustomed with, accepted
We can paint our own picture
Then have that come true.

Wanting something better
And praying for better days but this is just a little story
I didn't plan to go this deep
Look into my eyes
My story is bigger than you can understand.

Fostered

What are the odds of being fostered with love?
I mean really; what are the chances
That I'd get placed with someone sent from above
Not to be adopted
But to just be there.

Do tell what the odds are
Of being fostered with care
When looking at statistics
I'm sure it's clear to see
So, what are the odds
Of being fostered for me.

Seems unlikely
Not many are truly into it
They just know
Money for them
But how is this fair
To a child with nothing or no one there.

It wouldn't be fair to leave you
In this cruel world on your own
Doesn't everyone have parents?
To love and a place to call home.

But me, you see
I'm different
I was born into the system
Can't speak for myself
Don't even know what's happening.

All I know is today I can look back and see
How blessed I am that God covered me
Though never adopted
I was raised properly.

Had a mother, father, sisters
And even a brother
That was all close to me.

Didn't miss a meal
And I sure did love to eat
The state never paid them anything
My parents were the best thing that could ever happen to me.

A Mother's Heart

Pure and golden, shining and shimmering
Always ready, always willing
Hands to soothe the sorest places
The touches of a sweet Angel.

No matter where we were, she came in search
Of those in need ready to show them the way of life
Teaching, preparing, and wearing
Many hats around the house.

Keeping the values of family, education, growth
But first and foremost, instilling the values of the bible
As we go forward, we'll know our lives have been touched
Blessed with one of God's most precious mothers.

Nothing learned is in vain
Memories we carry in our hearts forever
But most of all the unforgettable
Unconsciously, bold love you gave us.

Rest on our guardian angel
Momma, we love you
Today, tomorrow, forever.

Need 'A (NITA)

Even when I try to explain
They don't understand
How bad I needed you.

These words could never describe
The pain deep inside
Hidden from the world
Afraid of what one might do.

But still I needed you
To show my truth
Strength and
Courage.

That came from
Not having you
There to guide me through
Is when I realized I needed you?

I needed you to be my truth
I needed you to know who I really am
A young girl lost, trapped without anyone
To talk too
Without anyone
To show me how to be a woman.

But now that you're here
I'm free from all my worries
I needed you.

Suicide

The mere attempt
When I tried to end my own life
I never speak on it
But its time
My silence be broken.

At age 16
I wanted to end it all
Life, bullies, rejection
Grabbed a razor
Cut deep
Mentally I'm scared forever from my attempt to end my life.

No longer will I accept it's not okay to be me
Just want to live this life through to the end
Suicide could have taken me away that day
Couldn't bear the mere pain.

I just wanted to be loved
Forgotten about or so I thought
Living a life full of questions
That no one could explain
That's how suicide almost took my life that day.

Hopeless and despaired
Wanting it all to end
So that I could
Be free and happy
But suicide wouldn't solve it.
If I had a purpose with a beautiful
Legacy to leave
So, picture me the same person
Eight short years later.

Two children
No longer alone
Still rejected for what I know
But I learned to
Accept myself for who I am
My story remains the same
That failed attempt at suicide has taught me the game.

Life has so much to offer
Even though you can't see it
Embrace all that comes your way.

Maybe the bullies were intimidated
Is one person worth ending your life?
My number one goal
Prove all the people who counted me out wrong.

Suicide almost took a mother and friend
But I couldn't see this back then

Suicide isn't worth it
You can live on
Life will get better.

If only you remain strong
Dedicated to those who have attempted suicide
Or are having suicidal
Thoughts hang in their life gets better.

Quanelias

To be sixteen and find out you got a baby on the way
Moved away from my parents only to see how that played out
Well, I lost my first, couldn't get that back
Learn to be careful what you ask for
At seventeen, I was pregnant again.

Ashamed
A little happy in my own way
Finally got back what was causing all my pain?
But wasn't aware of all it had to bring
Never stop to think.

Summer before my senior year
Wasn't prepared for what was coming but figured I'd face it anyway
Back to school and man that was something being rejected by someone who
Seemed so perfect while my legs were in the air
Had to ask myself was this even fair?

Didn't realize I had more to gain
Daddy dropping me off at appointments
While he drove around chilling

QPurpose

Couldn't believe this was my life
Seventeen and a baby inside me
Could no longer see my dreams.

Momma had to tell me one day
You made your mistake
Don't dwell, pick up and keep your pace.
Guess she didn't realize at seventeen
I was so unsure
Somehow, I managed and pulled through
By eighteen I gave birth; 7lb 13oz beautiful you.

Journey

Nothing simple about this path called life
It's different routes
That we can choose to take.

Seems like what matters is figuring it out
And that's rather quickly that I can say
You can lose yourself, but then would you go searching?
For whom you thought you were
But then again times are changing
So why go backwards
When you can always just move forward.

The pace of life seems so unfair
How to keep up when you're lost
But just want more.

Just come with me on this journey
Give it your best shot
Hope you did well and when
You're down keep your head held high.

Nothing like believing in yourself
A little hope that's what we all need
Setting a few goals, then going after them

Because we all know beyond the stars is where we want to be
Isn't no fear in the world can stop you
Just be bold and enjoy life's journey.

My beautiful loving daughter.
If ever you find yourself lost out here, just follow the words I have written here.
They'll take you far in life.
Love Mommy - Forever

Poison

Watch your mouth it's toxic to the soul
Got me feeling all weak
Sitting here out my mind amazed
About what's been going on.

You aint saying' nothin I'm enjoying tonight
Girl gone and pour me another drink
Hell, I already know I haven't been acting right.

I'm tripping been doing a lil sippin'
Even my son saying momma don't be drinkin
Got me feeling super weak so I reply "boy I'm grown what'cha mean "
But in reality, this booze is destroying me.

One more shot for me
I ain't drinking not one more
Then the liquor hit me
Why did he have to take my mother so soon from me?
So I go
One, Two, Three more shots
I'm done.

But the numb feeling keeping me calm

Out here acting a fool
My boo saying "Let's get some food "
I'm wasted try'na call home.

Stop and check the time it's only
Eight-fifty-three and that's a.m.
I mean p.m.
Seems everything is slurred.

Is it me or is this stuff
"Poisoning "
Because it got me super numb
My brain on pause
But I'm reacting.

People around me
Saying, "Girl you acting real dumb "
Why create such a drink for someone.

I can feel the vomit comin'
Just need some fresh air
I've come to realize that all the while long
We been drinking poison instead of what
Ya'll call fun
No truth comes from a part of a lie.

Without You

Picture life without you
Feeling like I'm learning something new
Most the time I'm stumbling to get by
But I manage and endure
Make a few steps towards a brighter future
Couldn't see this when I first lost you
All I seem to understand was pain.

But as my path becomes clear
I realize I have more to gain
You'll always be a part of me
And I know you feel the same.

I finally can accept Heaven
Simply had another precious angel to gain
In my heart I feel you near
What matters most was all the love you
had to share.

I pray that you keep watching over me no matter
where I go
Please stay close because you'll always be
My Guardian Angel the one I love the most.

Dedicated to my loving mother
Rest in Peace – May 20, 2014

Voice

Whenever I write
It comes from a place hidden deep down inside of me
Not premeditated
It comes rather naturally
From my heart that is where it starts.

The only time
I'm accepted
Know that
Whenever you read my story
It's not for the entertainment.

More about how
A young girl
Struggles to be accepted
After a constant
Battle at war
With confidence
Lack of self-love
I found myself lost in reality.

Identity issues make it hard for me to understand
Who is? So whenever I write
I see myself reflected as such
So strong

Not perfect.

An entire life of constant self-motivation
Pushing myself
Even when I had no one else
Always felt like life was a competition
I had to give my all
If I wanted to win it.

Understanding unclear
Now I thank my main man
As I shake his hand for always staying true and never turning his back
The man who taught me that if I work hard, I'd achieve big things
Excuse me, I went off on a limb.

As the memories run through my mind
I'm reminded of why I write because
The girl within is dying to be heard.

When I was younger
I promised myself I'd be my own voice
So whenever I write
I let my voice be heard.

Imagination

I figured you loved me
Not just taking advantage of
My submission to you
Figured it was perfect
Even when you warned me not to
I could have thought of one million reasons why I cared.

Still till this day
I find myself having minor dreads
Even with love, life seemed so right
But it wasn't that I loved, it's that I was growing
It wasn't the part about you showing me every reason I should've been against you
A love so bright it didn't deserve a dim light
If I had stepped back and observed, I would have said "Oh has got some nerve".

Allowing you to use, misuse, and then again abuse my feelings
I erupt into laughter as if I knew the feeling
Morphine was the drug that I seem to not get enough of

Everything around me seemed so numb

Caught up in a world where I was the painter
Boy your existence was measured by my mark
So how could my heart attach to a figment of my imagination?
When I created you.

Doubt

We all cry sometimes
No matter if inside or out
Because the fear within us
Can certainly cause a little doubt.

Why is it we fear the unknown?
But embrace what is ungodly
We'll go in circles for drama
Just to find out the why
And who did it
But the positivity can barely
Get a like or share.

Many will dislike me
Then try to avoid facing the fact
About this dark truth I'm sharing
But at the end of the day
Is it doubt or fear?

Dream

If they would've told me I'd be where I am today
"Ha"
You wouldn't like the look on my face
"Stay in school don't be no fool,
Girl leave them boys alone "
Just listen to what I'm saying
Better go make something out of yourself
Or they'll make out of you to better them.

Public housing living'
That's where we raising our children
Girl you got to be tripping
In the ghetto
C'mon think about it
They don't want them
To grow up
Wake up
Then make it up.

Gave me a dream, told me my rent was free
My son watched as the local thugs slang a few rocks
On the corner of the block
Is this what we've got to look forward to?
Women and even the girls twerking it all over social media

But what does that prove?

They told me girl stay in school don't be no fool
It's so hard being distracted because all the ones
with power sing about happens to be
Selective on secular
You can't filter what I see nor hear.

All I know is church Sunday morning was good
Come noon
All acting different
And it's got me tripping
Somewhat confused.

They gave me a dream but put limits on just how
big it could be
Told me "you might as well stop dreaming" once
that sperm was inside of me
Said that dreams weren't for people like me
Left me to wonder what did that mean?
So they went on to explain
You know, we're not trying to discourage you.

Abruptly blurted
"YOUNG AFRICAN AMERICAN SINGLE
MOTHERS WE MEAN"
Well ma'am they don't amount to nothin'
Seemed crazy but words will truly get to you
For a moment I quit dreamin'.

But that's when the statistics became true
Mean to tell me you're making money off the fact
that I lost hope
All these grants you're getting to help us
be better in life
But you rather tear us apart right from the start?

That small dream you sold
Then we're told
Sign here
These are the terms and conditions
"Give up and stop livin'. "

The choice was ours
So the contract was returned
Signed void and untrue.

"Trust in the Lord with all your heart; and lean not on your own understanding; in all your ways submit to him, and he will make your paths straight."
Proverbs 3: 5-6 (NIV)

Never give up on Dreamin!

Past

Oh how we miss you
Stayed such a short while
And now you're gone on down as
History...

Such a shame the new generation
Will never know your name
All they're concerned with is the cost of fame.

Times when meals meant we all gather as one
We pray, communicate and eat
Times where fathers took their place
Discipline, talks and even long prayers
Times where mothers would sew, cook, and clean.

But
Now
Seems like everybody on that Lean
I mean Gas if you know
What I mean?

Afraid of morals, values, ethics
Up on the internet acting reckless
Fights no longer happen
All they know is jumping

And keep it moving.

Isn't even afraid of being recorded
Ha, must think they're starting a movement
Until the police come knocking
Then a few charges are thrown.

Oh, is that how we define Fun?
Oh, Past how we miss you
It's so hard to dread on
Not enough leaders because
Everyone
Wants to be
One in the same.

Oh, Past please come back to us
Teach these young'ins
Of self-respect and dignity
I just logged off Facebook and you won't believe
what I seen.

Socially Oblivious

Today I did some thinking
Had to ask myself was I really being fair
Found myself plugged into social media
But disconnected from where I mattered most.

As I sat and watch my young children
In many ways cry out for attention
It began to remind me of how social media had blinded me
But I should take the blame.

Once I'm on it's like the content easily takes me away
Away from reality to another place
Find myself placing eyeballs on another girl's page
But the sad reality is who's busy raising my children?

Had to take a step back just to notice what's going on
So proud of the fellow member's accomplishing great things
Maybe they're living in reality while we're caught up on what's trending
More like socially oblivious.

The Waiting Room

As the needle pierced my skin
The thought of what if laid within
Was HIV Positive my Fate?
What had I done to get to this place?

All these posters to acquaint about knowing your status
And wrapping up to keep safe
Out in the lobby looking at different faces
Surely I wasn't the only one sitting there
With my mind in different places?

Nurse called me to the back
A negative HIV report slapped in my face
Wasn't a doubt in my mind on how to keep it this way?
Wrap it up
Get tested
Know your status or
HIV Positive could be my fate.

Empty

To go searching
But never find
To look high and low
But never know
To keep trying
But not be told
Even when you know
How could I find something?

When I'm empty down to my bones
To find what I'm in search of
To hold, hug and kiss this
The thought of me having and letting go
Even what I thought could be
Then again
It's not
Guess where that leaves me
Empty.

That Day

One day my mind changed
It's like my focus had become plainer
I thought of those babies I had to feed
Or how my mother was somewhere.

Sleeping in the heat
Something in my mind begin to wonder
It's like life was no longer a game.

I began to be more serious about
What I had to gain and changing my ways
Determination is a term I learned
That day.

Start

Start tomorrow or today
What's the difference?
If the people have no faith
Start today and help them change
Do your part and make sure it's from the heart
That's when they will see.

Remember abiding from these
Faith, Hope but Love remains the greatest
The only way to heal the broken
Is to be supporting and loving
Oh what a difference that will make
But first you must start.

Knowledge

Confused and living in a misunderstood world
Where it is acceptable to be ignorant
Then those with knowledge
Considered the noble
"Wise "
Still none choose to listen
Cause us black folk well, we know it all.

The need for education
On demand
Like life and death
Educate or die
Not in the flesh but in a sense where
Your existence
Unimportant because
Your lack of knowledge.

The bitter choices are to be
Ignorant
Ignore
What is one left to think?
This new world
So they say
Seems like
It's going to be men

"Downfall "
Still Misunderstood even while speaking facts.

They call you a leader
When in reality
Just a messenger
Warning the world
Wicked, dark, evil times
Headed our way
Let's not blame
Point fingers, or toes
One to another.

Be more open to
Embrace a fellow brother
Love will do us justice
Hate is no solution for our problem
Even the children
Angry shooting.

Fathers, mothers, sisters and brothers
There must be some
Miscommunication
Between God and his people.

"Speaks" Wisdom

How long will you love simplicity?
I understand you only live once
What about the future generations?
Watching each action carefully
So many fools who hate knowledge
And go their ways.

Be quiet and listen
From the streets you hear it
Crying
Even at the open gates its
Wisdom and knowledge
Just waiting to be received.

Valuable

You're worth
More than you know
So what are you settling for?
Is it to accommodate
A little boy
Who is yet
To become a man?

Who can appreciate all you have to offer him
So again my siesta
I ask
What are you settling for?
To be a slave to his entrapment
Years of tears
Crying out in pain
His love, your drug
But is it worth it?

You going to your grave
Not physically but
Emotionally
He's a parasite
Girl he's killing you
The sad part is
You can't seem to see the truth

So you carry on
Playing along
Russian roulette
The trigger is pulled
Boom!

Now you're done
Your life gone
Left lost and confused
Searching for something
Within someone else
The reality is
Girl you need to learn to love yourself.

Self-Discovery

I can see
So many women
Who need something
Unsure if it's love
Because deep inside
Falling apart.

Women
Wanting just a taste
Desperation
Killing us
Inside out
Unaware
Not really interested.

In what I have to say
The woman I was
Yesterday I can no longer
Stay
Picture us in search of something brighter
It's on the inside
Not out
Maybe it's time for me to
Love myself for who I am

No longer in search of happiness
Within a man.

But to appreciate my value
Because I love the person
I have begun to see
It's just a part of my self-discovery
That's why I love me.

For You

When the days seem longer
And the nights seem colder
May you never forget that this is
For you.

For you are beautiful
Uniquely created
A woman of noble character
You are the strength
That you need
Look inside
You will see
For you are gorgeous.

On your worst days just remember
That you My Dear
Are not alone
For You because
YOU ARE
Simply amazing
No one could compare
No matter what, remember
This is for You.

Awaken

Every morning I awake
To my harsh realities
I could allow it to tear me apart
Or be the new start.

Wasn't willing to look back on yesterday's
Mistakes
I chose to change
And forgive myself
Wasn't much I could say.

No, not perfect in anyway
Inside or out
All I wanted was something
Different
I could feel my soul crying, searching
In every door
Suddenly I found myself
Awaken.

Until Next Time

I hope that you have found strength, courage and joy in reading the poetry written throughout these pages.

Thank you for giving me the one, most priceless thing you will never get back and that is your time.

Thank you for taking the time to read my message and I pray this helps you no matter what you are faced with.

Look inside yourself and you will find all you need.

My Cousin, Mr. Shaque Jones

You are the reason this book is even coming into existence. If you had not stood behind me and begin to push me, I would still be at square one with this project.

More than you may know, I appreciate you. Not just for the photography, but it's like you found me at the perfect time.

We will call it destiny; I love you like a little brother I never had. Now whatever you set out to do, do it and be great at it. Know that I believe in you. I know you can and will.

Much Love,
Queen Shaena

An African American Young Woman

Twenty-Four Days of Reflections

December 1, 2015 - December 24, 2015

December 1, 2015

When I forgot about my ego, I allowed myself to soar. It was then my insides could feel the pain of my sister who was lost and hopeless. Was it the same pain I felt when I walked away? How could the world turn its back on such a beautiful sistah? Then my sistah, that's losing her Faith.

It's not what you have but how you use the resource that is within. Potential left untapped, your gifts that are going to waste but how do I explain myself to those who can't even see my face. Telling me that it's different for me, the expression on my face. Telling my sistahs the keys but they refuse to believe.

I think to myself of ways to get through to women who need to hear the truth. Then I remember that all of my thoughts are in my expressions. I sit at my computer searching for a way to relate. Not trying to come off in a misunderstood way. The direction of life forever changing so I begin to type, and the words flow. So easily but I second guess myself because I wanted the message to come off easier but then I remember this was as simple as it gets.

My sistah you have to come now with me - Rise UP and HAVE FAITH. Rise up my sistah, stay strong, walk until you can see the light. Never give up without a fight. Let your strength pull you through the good, bad and the misused. You have to preach, teach, and lead to show people the way; never just stand there and deteriorate.

December 2, 2015

Ma'am your daughter can't stay. Simply because you cannot afford to pay. It's just $16 dollars every week but when I reach down in my pocket, I realize they're empty. I'm strictly living off my faith. Standing there feeling like less of a woman because it's just a small fee, but they couldn't seem to understand my struggle as a young single mother.

The thoughts in my mind of how I must overcome to provide a better life for these young children. Glaring at the receipt then I look up out the window fighting back the tears that are trying to come through, thinking to myself, man, this is some bull...! I start work in just a few days; what am I supposed to do now? But I remember all the lessons on having faith so I pick up my child and walk out of the door feeling like I know that days will get better. Rushing home to fulfil my promise to myself that each day I'll write poetry; each day nothing more nothing less, the words quickly flowing from my heart then it hit me for the new level I was on I was facing a new devil.

The blessing coming is so big that the enemy doesn't want me to see, but some things you don't give up on. Laying in my bed, tears rushing from my eyes as I realize how much I've taken for granted. Filling these lines as my story unfolds, I think to myself what I have is more precious than gold.

So, I'll keep walking with my head held high and pride in my step because I'm not broken; I just haven't reached my best self yet!

December 3, 2015

I know you said I'm selfish but trust me I don't mean it. It was the first thing someone said to me in a while that made me think. Of all those times my selfish ways have been displayed, me blaming my friends and partners for my failure to compromise cause in my world it's my way or the highway.

I know you said I don't listen, but it's always been an issue. Just listen my voice never mattered and now I feel very empowered. I get the chance to speak and be heard so I'm sorry I cut you off. I know you couldn't finish your sentence, but I just thought of something more important my selfish butt just has to say.

I know you told me I need to be patient, but I swear I'm running out of time because I have yet to master the art of proper management. Somehow selfishly, I don't feel that it truly matters, which reminds me of how hardheaded I can be. It's easy to follow directions; do as I'm told but I was always a true rebel deep inside my soul.

I held the phone pouring out laughter because memories flooded my mind. Of the people I say I love most; hurting, but I digress. I am young and haven't figured life out, so I'll accept the challenge to step out of my shoes and see what I do wrong before you point a finger. Listening goes a long way but becoming unselfish and forgiving goes a long way. Not the complete answer but now you know where to start.

December 4, 2015

The thought of being next to something that seemed so complex running through my mind nonstop, trying to break barriers before the vision dies. Why does it seem that my dreams remain inside? How do I get them out to create a plan of action in order to make it happen? I'm feeling I need a major plan then execute it. I always picture something big because my vision is so great for now. I'm off to gain more knowledge and form a strategy to apply each day.

December 5, 2015

A lot goes in…a little comes out, as I reflect on life. I feel as though I'm in a daze reading through my poetry written over the past five days. I can see my story unfolding in its very own way. It's pretty unique how a writer can paint a picture in which an artist can paint…get my drift? Simplicity comes in the most natural way my self-expression I choose to share each day. I am, who I am, me, she, growing each day. Poetry time is over, and I must connect with those around me, but I'll be back shortly to share with you my personal reflections.

December 6, 2015

In the past few months it's like my why has been forgotten about. Today I did some reflecting, asking myself many questions. I wrote all these messages and now where do I go from here? I sat down reading after dinner, dessert, ironing clothes, doing hair, and bathing children. Feeling those words take me away to the place I wish to stay; it's my own world, I'm free to escape.

Now I'm wondering if my title matches the message. My voice sounds raspy as I recite words that at one point came straight from my soul. I felt like a stranger to my own words because I was on a different level, advanced and actually I smile inside and out as I reflect on who I was just a few months back… look at me now!

My name has changed and so has my story. I've found a way to make this all work out for me and not be ashamed of the story I bare. Reality calls and I must go. Remember to look for me tomorrow, I'll be back with more reflections.

December 7, 2015

This morning was hectic; waking up early and still being thrown for a loop of confusion. Went for a walk and some personal time communing with God. As I sit in Orientation to listen to policies and procedures. I'm thinking of other ways to succeed because honestly, I know I need the stability for my children. I just never pictured myself settling for less. I know I've got to do better, "it's a Jones thing", happening if I want something better.

December 8, 2015

As I sit next to a flickering candle, thoughts are racing through my mind… "What am I gonna do?" All I have is my faith. This was never about me but let me tell you how I felt breaking down in front of Koren. Back home was hectic but here I am trying to solve those issues. I felt so small, placing my pride to the side and carrying with me the load of my children on my shoulders.

My pockets are empty and the electricity way past due; now disconnected. I'm in need of an immediate blessing. I know God is going to provide; I know I need him. I'm not gonna flex, I saw this coming a mile away. Money is tight and bills are due, and the money didn't stretch enough to cover the lights last month. I'm just trying to get by. My mind wondered on my next move like, "Do I return home next year?" I've made it this far. I know I must get more focused.

I never want my children to feel the taste of having nothing. Am I wrong for wanting more? Right now, this mess don't feel sweet. I'm sitting here with this pen and paper shivering as I'm writing these words. I am asking God, "Please don't let my story go unheard." This struggle is tough, but I know it's about to get better, so I'll lay down now and close my eyes for some much-needed sleep. I know joy will come in the morning and sorrow don't last always.

December 9, 2015

Somehow my mind was going in circles last night, I didn't sleep at all. I woke up exhausted. My body didn't get any rest, but I pulled myself together and headed out to work. I was barely holding my eyes open but thinking of ways to make a difference. I'm not sad but the thoughts within are making me feel that I need to break free from poverty. This is not the life God intended for me, so I have to continue to put in my hours and grind not just on the clock but when I'm off building my brand.

Putting in effort to reap the rewards of my hard

work. I'll watch how my personal thoughts inside becomes a language for my brothers and sisters. I'm not the only one struggling I'm sure, many can relate. Will poverty continue to plague my life or will I make it out, beating the statistics? Either way, I'll keep writing, watching, and you will see among the stars is where I'm gonna be.
Sincerely - Drell J

December 10, 2015

As I sit here reflecting on one of the most life changing years I've yet to experience, I'm drawn to the special memories of when I was in and out of depression struggling to maintain my sanity. I remember the time when I allowed alcohol to suppress what I wasn't willing to express.

There was a time when my pockets were empty and I was ready to give up. I hid behind people to ease my pain. When I reflect on all those times, I remember that you were there by me. No matter what day or time I called, you answered and reminded me of just how important it was for me to hang in there and keep the faith. Here we are today…I'm receiving an award. You were the reason I remained strong in 2015.

I could never repay you and even if I could, the friendship we share is priceless and that's more than facts. I am so proud of all your accomplishments and how far you managed to come. Today is very special and I'm so happy for you today and forever. "You know what's funny?" I know you're sitting there with your eye's filled with tears ready to burst, so I'm going to my seat now because the waterworks are a tad much for me. Always remember you have a true friend in me. In 2016, I know we are well on our way towards greatness. It's our time, let's live on purpose!

Okay, now I'm done but before I go, I must say these things. Keep your head held high. The finish line is close now. Always remember to keep on that beautiful smile. Nothing is impossible. Sorrow will be over in a little while. When all else fails, enjoy some Kool Aid on the rocks, look up, and talk to God. I know this poem isn't much but it's a token of my appreciation to say thank you for an amazing year.
Dedicated to my best friend
Be'Jay "Betram" Major

December 11, 2015

As I sit at this computer, my mind is racing with so many ideas. Can't say I didn't see this coming. I know he's trying to discourage me right before my birthday. I've been stripped of everything this week. The only part of me still standing is my faith. I know God is about to come through. I don't know what's about to happen or why, but I know I've got my faith in God. As I sit here looking for answers, I'm gonna keep searching. All I know is there is no way I've taken these many losses just to stay down. I have to be on the edge close to a breakthrough. With my head held high and my pride to the side, "God," I ask Him, "What am I doing wrong? What are you trying to tell me in disguise?"

December 12, 2015

Some days I feel free and other days there are these triggers that go off and it's like everything links back to my mother abandoning me. She's not to blame. Someone told me a story one time about how it all went down. Sometimes I'm ready for the truth but it gets hard to accept. I'll probably never know what's real. The funny part about it is that it's her story to tell.

I just want to lay under my momma and have her brush my hair, cuddle, and just share in a moment of awe. I know, I know, it could be a dream come true to have her listen to my poetry as we laugh the night away. I opened my eyes and I'm brought back to reality, understanding that things may never change. Accept things as they are. Momma, you should know you are my mother and I am forever your loving daughter. You don't have to worry momma; promise it will get better.

December 13, 2015

Picture me receiving an award for "Motivator of the Year 2015" - it's funny. I've been at my lowest this year. I haven't had much money in my account. Hell, I don't even have an account. Welfare-living trying to take care of my children. I'm looking up to God, asking for His many blessings. Like what am I missing…it's a shame. I'm going through this because I'll work my ass off on anybody's job but trying to get an opportunity with that shoplifting charge from seven years ago has been a real hassle. But, I ain't gonna trip. I'm just going to keep going. Congratulations to myself. This is just the beginning of forever. Know I won't stop here, I have to keep going.

December 14, 2015

Midnight and I can't sleep. I'm an artist thinking of ways that I can eat. Tears from within crying to be heard but caged behind those bars, the ones that shackle me. Validation I mean. See, I don't know who I am. Confidence is something I'm learning. I walk past a mirror never once turning into it. Deep down inside I'm dying because this voice I carry just needs to be heard, the voice of my people who struggle like myself. So I forget my pride and run to soar with the eagles because all I ever wanted was a damn brighter day.

No, you could never imagine the pain I felt watching my momma suck that poison from that pipe as the tears streamed from my eyes. Her demon within asking me, her child, "Are you okay?" Knowing darn well he was to blame for my family's pain. I tell myself daily that I don't grind for myself, it's for my family. It's 12:00am in the morning and I'm just up thinking...

December 15, 2015

Whenever I explain my struggle, I don't know if they feel me because it's my pain; they can't possibly agree with me...my hustle, my ambition, going crazy. What will it take to just make a dollar a day in my own way? I want to get away from here and escape. I ain't never coming back because I don't like the way this feels inside. Driving me insane, sometimes I think I'm the only one facing obstacles or I'm the only one who want it as bad as I do. Excuse my French but @!@@!! going back where I am right now my heart feels so numb to the pain. I can feel inside trying to get by but each step forward is five pushes backward trying to lay a sturdy foundation so I can take my children on a paid and full vacation. I owe them much more in life than to struggle just to get by so I'm looking at the clock and counting the days until it's my time but, in the meantime, I'll keep working.

December 16, 2015

You have stolen my mother's soul. She's too dependent to even let you go. You took my sister in childhood causing her to grow up young. Robbed me of my innocence and I didn't even know your name. You made my mother take beatings she didn't deserve. You've cursed us and left us broken and still you haunt us, and we've never even spoken. I wonder sometimes if you care that you left generations broken. Our mother at one point was different but her relationship with you has her tripping. You're getting stronger with that grip.

I feel my emotions getting weaker. You ain't my mother's friend, yet momma won't let you go. She depends on you to get by and she can't even see through your lies. You've got her tricked up in her mind. Sometimes I wonder how you're so close to my mother and we've never crossed paths but then again, I do know your name. My childhood was destroyed the day my mother touched crack cocaine. I hate you so bad but you're just a drug and you'll never know my name! *The heartbroken daughter fostered*

December 17, 2015

Airport adventure: The life of a misfit trying my hardest to get it at the airport. Making observations, silently watching, but excitedly waiting thinking about the day this will be my way of life. I love the thought of air way travel; watching airplanes arrive and depart. Thinking of ways, I can start on my journey to something new. Sitting in the parking lot, watching. I just love the idea of traveling. So quick airport adventures, a place that's always busy, traffic in and traffic out. People arriving and some departing. We look around and realize the airport is full.

December 18, 2015

On this date, we understood how important it is to give back as we sat at the charity event on the "receiving" end. Giving back is important clearly when so many people are in need. I checked my surroundings so I could see just if I am really in need. So, I think to myself, as I sit there just understanding what I can do to give back. I'll be giving something in return.

December 19, 2015

As I sit here with one of the few women, I consider a friend, I escape from the past two weeks which have truly been a nightmare. Whenever I surround her, the energy is so positive. She doesn't even know how whenever I mention her name, I consider her my friend. From the city I'm still new too. But I'll let her speak now because I'm done.

Shaena Jones

In my feelings,
Feeling all blue
She's braiding hair which I consider her a pro
But yet her self-reflection won't let it show
Me, oh my oh, what a mess
I wish I could do better cause I'm not the best,
But with God's direction I will pass the test

Because the teacher is always quiet during the test.
Teleshia Wesley

December 20, 2015

Reflecting over the week, I would say there were some ups and some down moments, but it ended pretty good. As I sat down last night enjoying good company, I realized it's not about what you have or the friends you say you don't have. It's about living in the present moment and enjoying the loved ones we do have around us.

December 21, 2015

School's out, I know what that means. Both kids are home with me.

Sitting around thinking what can we do. Excited about the holidays.

School is finally out and the children's hearts are filled with joy as they understand that Christmas is near.

December 22, 2015

Curious, misunderstood. Boldly standing in the shadows of darkness.

Waiting for a moment to emerge. A voice I know needs to be heard, one of a queen walking in light. Treading so lightly footsteps heavily impacting the earth. She the Queen walks the earth roaming for people to heal, places to see and things to explore.

Twenty-Four Days of Reflections

December 23, 2015

On the road again headed to the place I call home. The excitement of having my birthday so near makes me feel awesome inside. Ready to celebrate. Looking out at the open road thinking to myself how proud I am of how far I've managed to come. My thoughts were no longer the same as they were before. This was it, the last day I'll be this young but still older than ever before. So I think to myself freely reflecting on how much I have accomplished. Just me, the kids and the open road.

December 24, 2015

It's my day today and I'm excited. Spent the night last night with my best friend. She was baking a cake when I arrived. I woke up on the bathroom floor. Trying to understand what happened. It's my birthday and I'm gonna celebrate. Happy birthday Love. Happy birthday love. I keep telling myself there is nothing else to be but happy.

Deep down inside I was so worried about bills. How I was going to get a new tag registration? I attempted to hide it. I hate it when I have to lie to myself.

This mess seems so unreal. Like I'm in a daze. I don't know if it was the past few months that lead me to this point or if I just lost control. Today I got my makeup done, compliments of my best friend.

It's my birthday. As my day begins the love and

affection my family and friends poured out towards me was just overwhelming. I just have to say thank you again to everyone who made my year so amazing. I didn't really have a poem to write for today, but I had a story to share. As the day begins, I was overly excited. I was going to have dinner with my family and friends at Logan's; man, I just love the bread and butter they have.

As the day went on, I unfortunately had to find a different location because I hadn't made any reservations and they had two parties booked for the time I wanted. I immediately Googled a restaurant and found O'Charley's thinking to myself I really don't want to go there but I will. I made reservations and went about my day meeting up with Loko to have my hair flat ironed.

As we sat there laughing and enjoying each other it begins to storm. Inside I felt saddened but figured the day must go on. Checking my Facebook many of my family and friends backed out at the last minute. I refused to let this get to me. Carrying on with my day, I rushed through the storm to take my sister to the store. It's 6:00 pm and I'm running late to my own dinner.

As my phone rings, I'm thinking what do I say? It's Tina and she has arrived. I said, "Pookie, I'm running late, I'm coming. I'm not even dressed, and my legs aren't even shaved. I have to drop my sister off then drive all the way to my best friend's house, to shower, shave and get dressed."

After dropping my sister off I managed to run into two different potholes that were full of water. I begin to slow down and take my time; I thought to myself that time was not going to run out. Upon arriving to my best friend's house, I ran through the door up the stairs and again my phone rings, its Tina. She says, "Man where ya'll at?" I said, "We're coming, I'm so sorry. Well I'm going to Wal-Mart before they close."

I hung the phone up and thought to myself for a moment what today meant to me. I was rushing so I slid on my dress and asked my best friend were my legs noticeable that I hadn't shaved. I oiled them up and headed out of the door. When we arrived at the restaurant, I was surprised. I hadn't been to this restaurant since the day of my high school graduation back in 2009 and here it is 2015; we meet again.

I thought I had called Cheddars Casual Café. My phone had died and wouldn't even charge so I was unplugged from the world and facing reality. At the dinner was me, Brittany, Tina and Sierna. We all sat around the table, gathered in laughter. Brittany and Tina were telling me how proud they were of how far I came; everyone giving me advice on different things. As I did some personal reflecting, I realized how much I had done over the past few years and how I had gotten by. But the most important thing is I met myself that night in O'Charley's.

To my friends, this one is for you: Brittany, Shatina, Sirena. You will never know how thankful I am that you joined me and made my birthday just that much more special with the very therapeutic dinner. I wish you guys so much happiness, love, success and joy in the New Year. Slow down, be patient, keep your eyes open, for the road ahead holds many undiscovered secrets.

What I Wish I Knew At Twenty-Four?

Life goes on.
Girl get all the help you can get.
Get up and fight. Why you crying?
Look how far you came.
Everybody is not able baby.
Mind your business.
Everyone is not meant to stay.

I moved away from home with two kids and no job. If I can do it, I know you can make it. Life is not easy. Stop rushing. Girl, PROTECT YOURSELF. JUST BECAUSE HE CAME DOES NOT MEAN HE REMAINS. SPEND TIME ALONE. We want everyone to do for us but what are we willing to do for ourselves?

When I got to Atlanta in 2015, I moved into my apartment; I had no money. It cost $350.00 to turn on my lights. I phoned my dad and he was not even trying to hear it. He instantly told me he would think about it but I knew it was a sure no! So, what did I do? I cried about it first but then I thought about it; what was I to do? Forget it, I had to survive so I pawned the title to my car and got $600.00. I didn't even pawn the title in Atlanta, I had to drive all the way home! I felt so accomplished when I dropped off that $350.00 to Fairburn utilities. It was a lot of money, but I had to make it happen.

I was in Atlanta with no job; life was tough. I received some welfare and the ladies where I was assigned to receive unemployment services believed in me. One day one of them pulled me to the side and asked, "What are you doing here and why didn't I have a job?" They told me that I was smart, spoke well, and carried myself well. What she didn't know was although I spent time job searching and I learned so much while in the program, I was busy writing books. I had no idea on how to put a book together. Even though I am an avid reader, I felt that I was just DREAMING. I began searching, so I spent a lot of time alone. I took nature trail walks and spent time in the library. At the unemployment office, I worked on my book and printed copies. Often, I sneaked to the printer to grab my copies while no one was watching.

Something in me wanted to win and I wasn't going to stop until I succeeded. Writing became my outlet.

I erased distractions so that I could focus on writing. I wrote while facing divorce, about divorce, "crazy"! I wrote about my past life when I didn't even feel worthy of telling the story. After the children were in bed and I was alone, my heart flowed, and I put that information to paper. Meditation was a great remedy that I learned. It's something about a struggle that will make you "hungry", that's what I felt like. For years I was auto piloting through life. I am now a grown woman looking in the mirror; I didn't know myself.

I was hoping, praying, and wishing things would change while giving all I could to others. Writing is not something everyone can do; it's a gift. I'm not just a writer, I'm a storyteller. I live, I see, I hear, I endure, and then I give an account for what has taken place. I tell the world the story through my perspective. There is no way you can get good at something unless you study…I mean really study. You must devote your time to it and dive so far into it that you give it your all. DREAMING is nothing without action. I wrote my first book nearly a year or two before it was published and the information in this book is older than that one. It's one thing to have a plan but to put the plan into motion is something separate. We must allow ourselves time, space, and energy to grow, learn, and develop.

What's Happening 24?

We exist daily within a 24-hour period. At the end of 24 hours a new cycle begins. As I look inward at the age of 24, I see a new beginning. Looking into my life at 24, I am a different person. What I have seen and what I have experienced; life was amazing.

Once I was on such a thrill ride, seeking something I thought I was missing. In the middle of the thrill, I had a wakeup call, a real reality check.

I had to ask myself, "Girl, what are you doing? You're out here in this dangerous world acting as if you aren't risking your entire life. Instantly, my eyes opened. I was chilling with this guy at that time and immediately I asked him to leave. He was lost for words because we were having such a good time. I changed my environment because out of nowhere, I was overcome with fear. I thought to myself, "He could kill me and my kids and no one would know because I didn't know anyone in Atlanta."

As soon as he left, I started crying and praying, "Lord, what am I doing?" I was struggling with my abandonment demon; I thought I couldn't walk alone. What the hell was I thinking about inviting random men into my life? I knew nothing about them and no, it wasn't always sexual. It was about keeping someone close so I wouldn't be alone. Strangers! Lord, what danger was I facing? One of the men had the audacity to try and move in on me, I had to get rid of him too. Oh, the adventures I have experienced.

I made a decision to clear out my space and keep a clear conscious. After the wakeup call, things were different. I had to get my attention centered and recharged. There was something in me that was pushing me to reach higher. I renewed the vision for my book, "The Journal of My Journey, "a story about being a girl and the challenges I overcame.

There will always be a generation that will need someone like you and I with experiences, stories and testimonies to share to encourage others. When we share our stories, we walk in faith and in understanding. Something about speaking our truth we awake from a comfortable sleep post.

January	Asked my husband to leave my house.
February	Got a DUI.
	Signed up for CNA class.

What's Happening 24?

March	Found out I was pregnant. Started CNA class.
April	Lost the baby. Started clinical for CNA class.
May	Graduated from CNA class. My mom passed. My husband went to jail.
June	Failed one part of my certification test. Moved from my apartment to live with my cousin. Retook failed part of certification and passed the test.
July	Living with cousin and job searching.
August	Got first CNA job with the state. Lights got cut off because someone turned them off.
September	Working 3:00pm - 11:00pm
October	Hubby and I communicated by letters. Hubby is going to prison.
November	Started reading. Decided to move to Atlanta.
December	Worked a lot of OVERTIME Celebrated 25!!

"The Evolution of time is beautiful. It's all about trusting the process and allowing things to happen. We grow through our experiences and learn through them. Through grace, we come out better on the other side."

What's Happening 24?

Life is way too short to be caught living lies and being sad about decisions you made. Get up and FIGHT on!

Let's chat soon.

Love always,

Queen

Shaena and Biological Mom (1991)

Thanksgiving 1992

Mom, Dad, and Shaena (NJ 2012)

Shaena & Mother
Harris Family Reunion
2013
Augusta, Georgia

Look what I found
when I unpacked

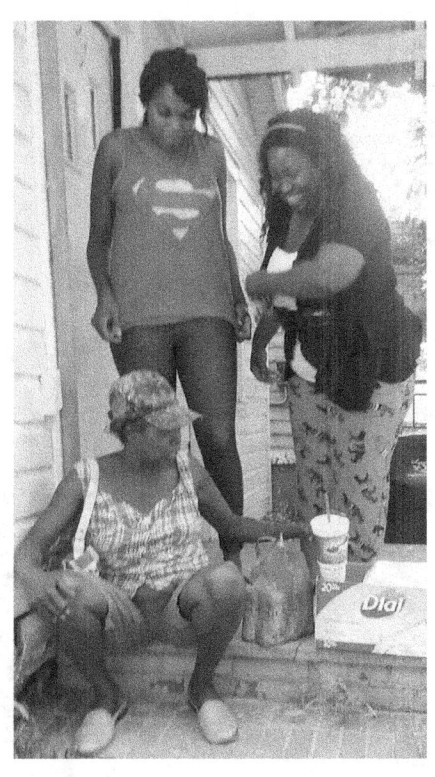

Sheana, biological mother and oldest sister (Summer 2014)

*My loving mother
Rest in Peace -
May 20, 2014*

High School Senior Year

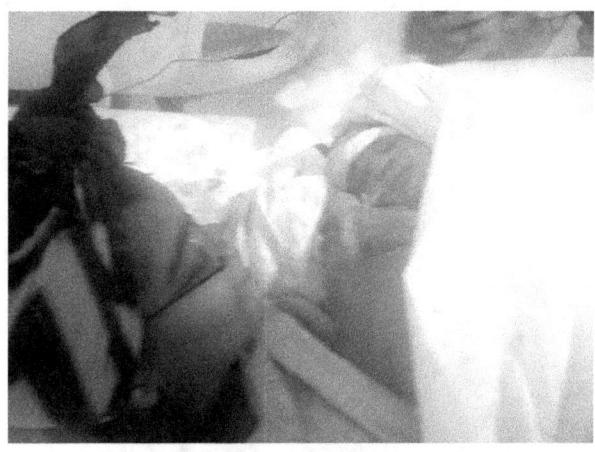

My First Born Quanelias J (March 6, 2009)

Quanelias & Shaena (Winter 2013)

Quanelias & Shaena (Winter 2013)

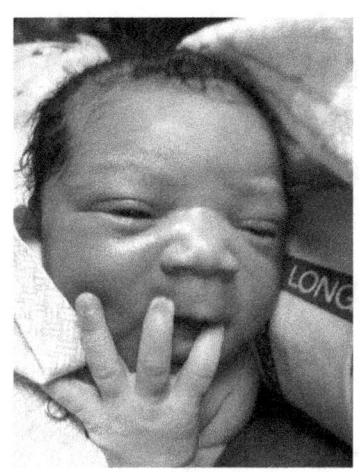 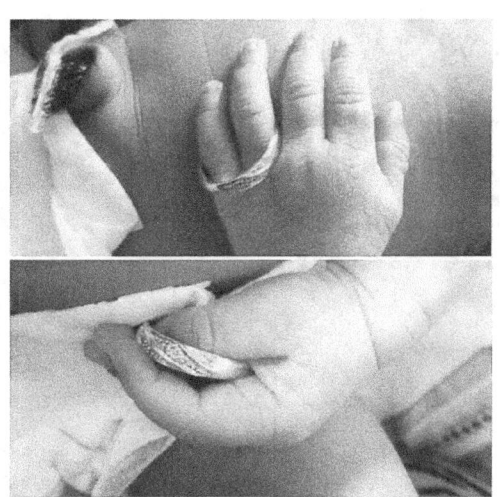

Journey (2013) *Journey holding Mom's Wedding Band*

P.O. Box 453
Powder Springs, Georgia 30127
www.entegritypublishing.com
info@entegritypublishing.com
770.727.6517

www.ingramcontent.com/pod-product-compliance
Lightning Source LLC
Chambersburg PA
CBHW071020080526
44587CB00015B/2432